Let's Bake a Cake

Let's Bake
a Cake

HELEN DREW and ANGELA WILKES

DK

How to use this book

Let's Bake a Cake shows you how to bake lots of delicious cakes and pastries. Below are the points to look out for when using this book, and a list of things to remember.

Cook's tools

Illustrated checklists show you which tools to have ready before you start each project.

The ingredients

All the ingredients you need for each recipe are shown clearly to help you check that you have the right amounts.

Step-by-step

Step-by-step photographs and clear instructions tell you exactly what to do at each stage of the recipe.

Cook's rules

- Only bake when there is an adult there to help you.

- Read each recipe before you start to make sure you have everything you need.

- Always wash your hands, wear an apron, and roll up your sleeves before you start.

 •Always wear oven mitts when picking up anything hot, and when putting things into or taking them out of the oven.

- Never leave the kitchen when stove top burners are turned on.

- Always make sure that you turn the oven off after you have finished baking.

A DK PUBLISHING BOOK

Editor Sarah Johnston
Designers Caroline Potts and Adrienne Hutchinson
DTP Designer Almudena Díaz
Managing Editor Jane Yorke
Managing Art Editor Chris Scollen
Production Ben Smith
Photography Dave King

First American Edition, 1997
2 4 6 8 10 9 7 5 3 1
Published in the United States by DK Publishing, Inc.
95 Madison Avenue, New York, New York 10016
Visit us on the World Wide Web at http://www.dk.com

Copyright © 1997 Dorling Kindersley Limited, London
Projects originally published in *My First Cook Book* and *My First Baking Book*
Copyright © 1991, 1991 Dorling Kindersley Limited, London

A catalog record is available from the Library of Congress.

ISBN 0-7894-1560-7

Color reproduction by Colourscan
Printed and bound in Italy by L.E.G.O

CONTENTS

LITTLE CAKES

Little cupcakes are simple and quick to make. Here you can see everything you will need to make about ten regular and ten small plain or cherry cupcakes. If you wish to make more, you will have to double or triple the amounts of ingredients shown. Don't forget that you will need more frosting, too!

On the next four pages there are lots of exciting ideas for frosting and decorating all your cupcakes.

You will need

2 eggs

6 candied cherries

½ cup (100 g) soft margarine

½ cup (100 g) granulated sugar

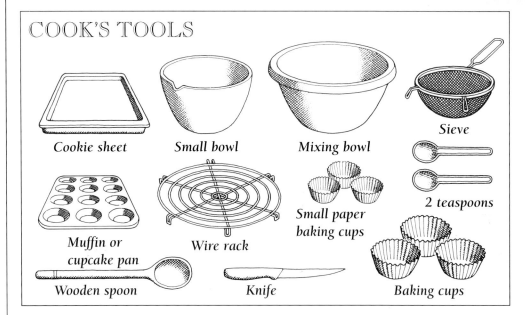

COOK'S TOOLS

Cookie sheet

Small bowl

Mixing bowl

Sieve

Muffin or cupcake pan

Wire rack

Small paper baking cups

2 teaspoons

Wooden spoon

Knife

Baking cups

What to do

1 Set the oven to 350°F (180°C). Put the larger baking cups in the muffin pan and the small cups on the cookie sheet.

2 Sift the self-rising flour into the mixing bowl. Add the margarine and the sugar to the flour.

3 Break the eggs into the bowl. Beat everything together with the wooden spoon until the batter is soft and creamy.

4 To make cherry cupcakes, cut the candied cherries into small pieces with a sharp knife* and stir them into the cake mixture.

5 Put two teaspoonfuls of batter into each large paper cup and one teaspoonful into each small one.

6 Bake the small cupcakes for 10-15 minutes and the regular ones for 20-25 minutes. Then put them on a wire rack to cool.

¾ cup (100 g) self-rising flour

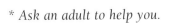

* Ask an adult to help you.

7

FROSTING CUPCAKES

You can make lots of different frostings for your cupcakes. Here you can find out how to make chocolate, white, and pink buttercream frostings, and how to color ready-made fondant icing and mold it into shapes. Look on the next two pages for decorating ideas.

½ cup (100 g) very soft butter

⅓ cup (100 g) ready made fondant icing

You will need

2 tablespoons cocoa powder

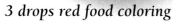

3 drops red food coloring

1¾ cups (215 g) confectioners' sugar

COOK'S TOOLS

Mixing bowl

2 small bowls

Wooden spoon

Sharp knife

Knife

Sieve

8

What to do

1 Put half the butter into the mixing bowl and cut it into small pieces. Beat it with the wooden spoon until it is creamy.

2 Sift ¾ cup (125 g) of confectioners' sugar into a small bowl. Mix the sugar into the butter a bit at a time until creamy.

3 Put half of the frosting into another small bowl and beat in the red coloring to make it pink. (The other half is white frosting.)

Fondant icing

4 To make chocolate frosting, use ¾ cup (125 g) of sugar and the cocoa powder and follow steps 1 and 2 above.

1 To make pink fondant icing, add three drops of red coloring to the fondant. Mix it until the color is even.

2 Make a roll of fondant for the elephant's trunk and shape flat circles for its ears. Make pig's ears from flat ovals of fondant.

Cakes with faces

1 Peel the paper cups off the cupcakes. Arrange the regular and small cupcakes together to make faces with ears or noses.

2 Frost the bottom and sides of a small cupcake and stick it on top of a regular cupcake covered with the same colored frosting.

3 When you have frosted all your cakes, give them faces by decorating them with candies before the frosting sets.

FUNNY FACES

Little cakes are lots of fun to make and they look really bright and colorful. You will need to look for all sorts of different candies to use for decoration. Copy the butterflies, soldier, teddy bear, elephant, and other funny face cupcakes shown here, or experiment with some ideas of your own!

Why not try making funny faces that look like your family and pets for a special family meal or party?

You will need

Licorice pieces

Red licorice "string"

Licorice strips

White chocolate chips

Chocolate chips

Candied cherries

White chocolate buttons

Chocolate buttons

Candy-covered chocolates

Chocolate sprinkles

CHERRY CUPCAKES

Eat your cherry cupcakes as they are, or frosted and decorated with candy.

Pieces of candied cherry

BUTTERFLIES

Cake wings

Butter-cream frosting

Cut a circle out of some small cupcakes and then cut the circles in half to make wings. Fill the hole in the cupcakes with buttercream frosting and put a wing on each side.

PIG

Chocolate chip eyes

Pink fondant ears

Chocolate chip nostrils

Red candy-covered chocolate tongue

SEAL

Chocolate chip and white chocolate button eyes

Chocolate sprinkle fur

Licorice whiskers

SOLDIER

Chocolate sprinkle-covered cake for a hat

Red licorice eyebrows

Chocolate chip and yellow chocolate eyes

Candied cherry nose

Red licorice mouth

Licorice chin strap and mustache

Small cupcake cut in half with pieces of chocolate buttons for ears

Chocolate chip and yellow candy-covered chocolate eyes

RACCOON

White chocolate button and liquorice nose

ELEPHANT

Pink fondant circles on small cupcakes for ears

White chocolate chip tusks

Pink fondant trunk curled up on a small cupcake

TEDDY BEAR

Red candy-covered chocolate nose

Chocolate sprinkle covered snout

Chocolate button ears

White chocolate chip and licorice eyes

DOG

Chocolate chip eyes

Licorice nose

Chocolate sprinkle whiskers

Red candy-covered chocolate tongue

Chocolate chip eyes

SURPRISE CAKE

For birthdays, parties, and other celebrations it is nice to make a special cake. Or you can make a cake just because you want to surprise someone. Here is a recipe for a light and delicious sponge cake that you can decorate however you want. You can find out how to frost and decorate it in different ways.

You will need

⅔ cup (150 g) softened butter

⅔ cup (150 g) all-purpose flour

Making the cake

1 Set the oven at 350°F (180°C). Rub some butter around the insides of the two cake pans thoroughly.

2 Put the softened butter and sugar in the mixing bowl. Beat them with the wooden spoon until the mixture is pale and creamy.

3 Beat the eggs in a small bowl. Add them to the butter and sugar a little at a time, stirring the mixture until it is smooth.

3 eggs

¾ (150 g) granulated sugar

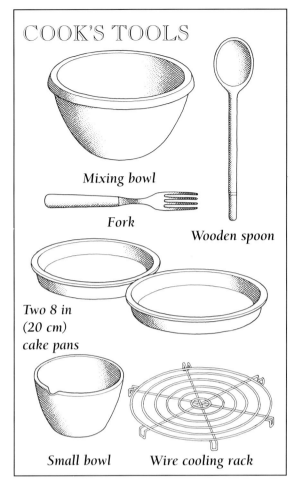

1½ teaspoons baking powder

4 Sift the flour and baking powder into the mixture and mix well. The cake mixture should be soft and light.

5 Pour half of the cake mixture into each pan and smooth it until level. Place the pans in the oven for 20 to 25 minutes.

6 The cakes are done when risen, brown, and springy in the middle; remove from pans and place them on a wire rack to cool.

PICTURE CAKE

This cake was filled and topped with chocolate buttercream frosting and decorated. Copy the picture of the Sweet Hen or make up one.

You will need

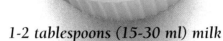

1-2 tablespoons (15-30 ml) milk

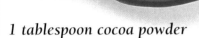

1 tablespoon cocoa powder

6 tablespoons softened butter

1½ cup (150g) confectioners' sugar

Frosting the cake

1 Put the butter in the bowl and cut it into small pieces. Beat it with the wooden spoon until it is soft and creamy.

2 Sift the confectioners' sugar and cocoa powder into the bowl a little at a time, mixing them with the butter. Stir in the milk.

3 When the cakes are cool, spread half the frosting on one then put the other cake on top and spread the rest of the frosting on it.

Turn the page for another decorated cake.

Arranging the Candy Hen

4 Now decorate the cake. Press the candy firmly into the frosting. Start with the border, do the nest, and arrange the hen last.

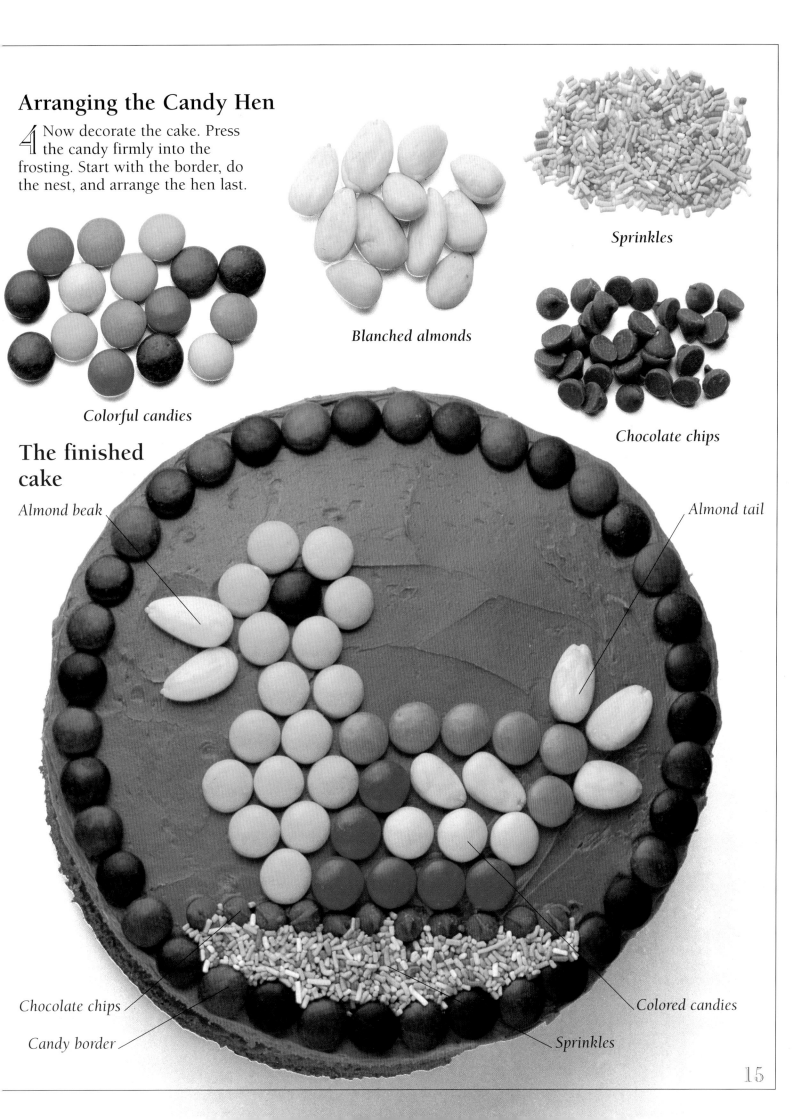

Colorful candies

Blanched almonds

Sprinkles

Chocolate chips

The finished cake

Almond beak

Almond tail

Chocolate chips

Candy border

Sprinkles

Colored candies

15

Frosted Flower Cake

This cake is filled with jam and topped with frosting and crystallized grapes and flowers. Real flowers are for decoration only. Use marzipan, as shown here, if you want to eat them. The flowers and fruit take 2 to 3 hours to dry, so allow enough time for this.

You will need

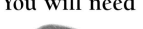

1 egg

White frosting, using 1½ cup (175g) confectioners' sugar and 3 tablespoons of hot water

What to do

1 Crack the egg over a bowl. Pour the yolk from one half of the shell to the other, so that the white slips into the bowl.

2 Whisk the egg white until it is frothy. On a wire rack placed over a plate, paint the flowers and grapes with egg white.

3 Sprinkle a layer of sugar over the flowers. Dip the grapes into the sugar to coat them. Then leave the flowers and grapes to drain.

COOK'S TOOLS

Pastry brush

Teaspoon

2 Bowls

Knife

Whisk

Wire rack

4 Spread each cake with jam and sandwich them together. Make the frosting* and spread it over the top of the cake with a wet knife.

5 Arrange the flowers, petals, and grapes on the cake so that they will stick to it before the frosting starts to set.

*Sift the confectioner's sugar into a small bowl. Add the water a little at a time, mixing with the sugar to make a smooth pas

Bowl of granulated sugar

Small marzipan flowers

Grapes

Apricot jam

The finished cake

Crystallized grapes

Crystallized flowers

Crystallized petals

Pastry In A Pan

Puff pastry* is lots of fun to make since it puffs up to two or three times its size when you bake it. Here and on the next five pages, you can find out how to make and decorate lots of different puff pastries. The ingredients shown below will make about five spiders, snakes, puffs, and éclairs, and lots of worms.

You will need

¾ teaspoon salt

7 tablespooons (100 g) butter

1¼ cup (150 g) plain flour

4 eggs

1 beaten egg

1 cup (250 ml) water

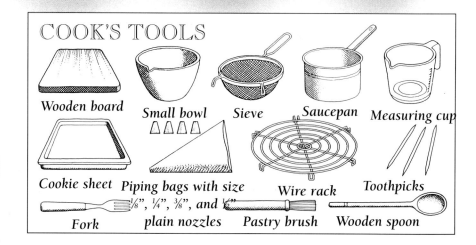

COOK'S TOOLS

Wooden board   Small bowl   Sieve   Saucepan   Measuring cup

Cookie sheet   Piping bags with size ⅛", ¼", ⅜", and ½" plain nozzles   Wire rack   Toothpicks

Fork   Pastry brush   Wooden spoon

18

*In France this is called choux pastry.

What to do

1 Set the oven to 400°F (200°C) Grease the cookie sheet. Sift the flour into the small bowl.

2 Put the water, salt, and butter into the pan. Heat them gently until the butter has melted and the mixture begins to bubble.

3 Remove the saucepan from the heat and set it on a wooden board. Add all the flour to the mixture at once.

4 Beat the mixture vigorously until it pulls away from the sides of the saucepan. Let it cool for one to two minutes.

5 Beat the eggs in the small bowl. Add them to the mixture a little at a time until it is smooth and shiny.

6 Put a nozzle* onto the piping bag. Put the bag in the measuring cup and fold its top over the sides. Spoon in the mixture.

7 When the bag is full, twist the top to close it. To start piping, squeeze the pastry down through the nozzle.

8 Pipe your shapes onto the greased cookie sheet and brush them with beaten egg. Bake them for 20 to 25 minutes, until golden.

9 Remove the shapes from the oven and prick each one with a toothpick. Place the shapes on a wire cooling rack .

*Turn the page to see which nozzle to use to pipe each shape.

LIGHT AS AIR

You can pipe puff pastry into any shape you like. Follow the instructions at the bottom of the page to make spiders, snakes, worms, puffs, and éclairs. When the shapes are cool, fill them with whipped cream and top them with the chocolate frosting shown opposite.

You will need

1 cup (100 g) semisweet chocolate

1 cup (100 g) confectioners' sugar

PUFFS

To make puffs and spiders' bodies, use the ½ inch nozzle and pipe small mounds onto the cookie sheet.

SNAKES

Use the ⅜ inch nozzle to make the snakes. Start at the head of the snake and pipe a wiggly line for its body.

SPIDERS' LEGS

Pipe the spiders' legs using the ⅛ inch nozzle. Make four left legs and four right legs for each spider.

WORMS

These are piped with a ¼ inch nozzle. Pipe the worms as though you are writing commas.

blespoons (25 g) butter

1¼ cup (300 ml) double cream

3 tablespoons water

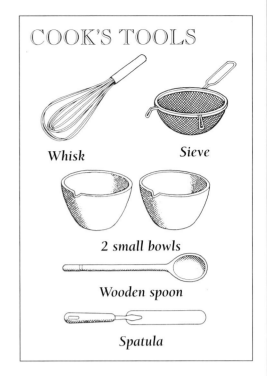
What to do

1 Whisk the cream in a small bowl until it is thick and fluffy. Cut the puffs and éclairs in half and spoon the cream into them.

2 Cut the butter and chocolate into pieces. Put them in the saucepan and stir them together over low heat until they melt.

ÉCLAIRS

Eclairs are made with the ½ inch nozzle. Pipe 2 in (5 cm) lines of pastry for mini éclairs and 4-in (10 cm) lines for big ones.

3 Stir in the water. Remove the mixture from the heat. Sift the sugar and then add it to the mixture. Stir until smooth.

4 Spread frosting along the buns, éclairs, and snakes with a spatula. Dip the worms in the frosting with your fingers.

21

PUFF PARADE

Here are some ideas for decorating your puff-pastry shapes. The spider's web was made by piping some of the chocolate frosting onto a large white plate. Try piping other animals or even a puff dragon for a special occasion or party.

The finished cakes

Raisins

Red licorice

Sprinkles

Rainbow sprinkles

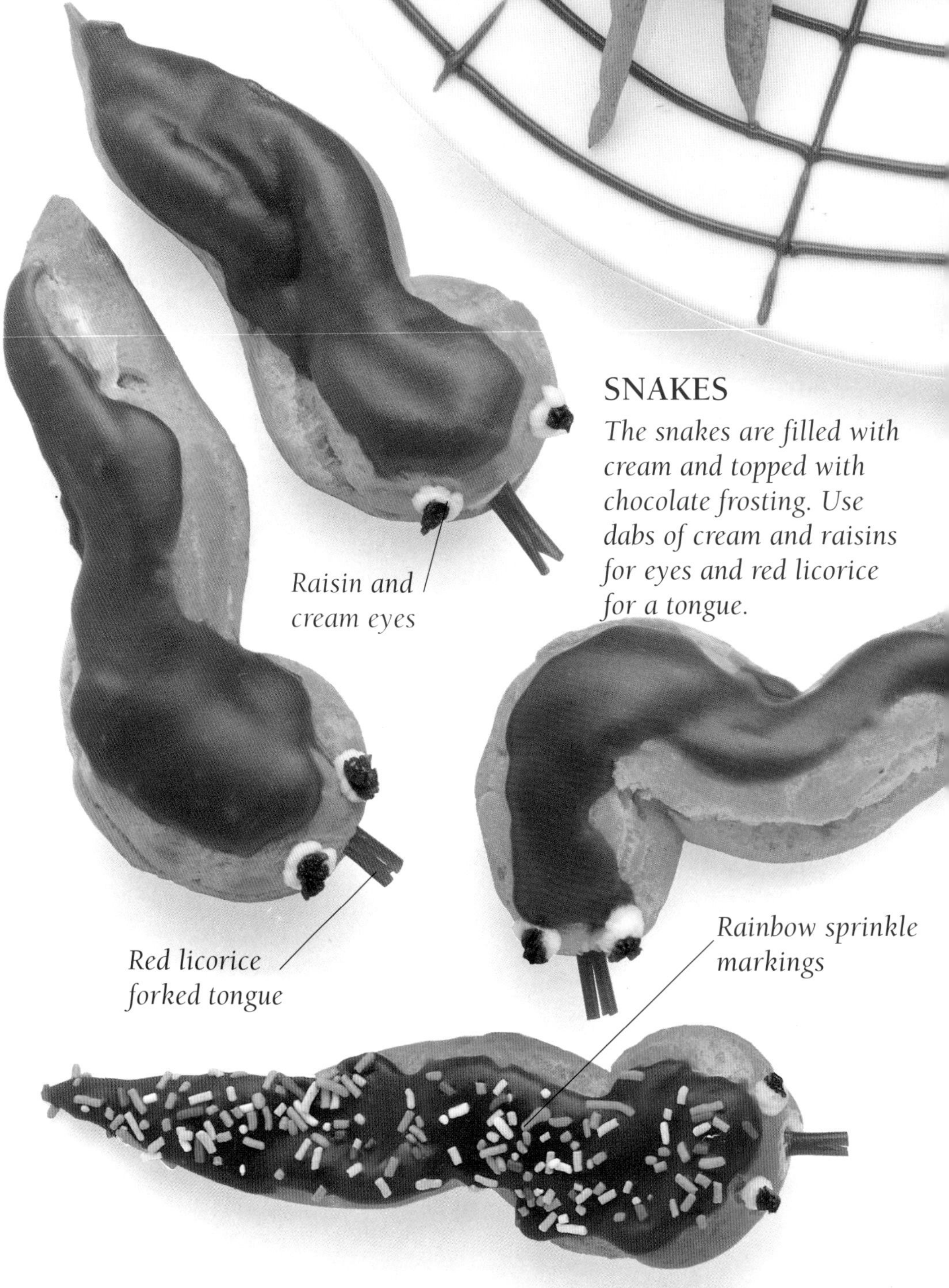

SNAKES

The snakes are filled with cream and topped with chocolate frosting. Use dabs of cream and raisins for eyes and red licorice for a tongue.

Raisin and cream eyes

Red licorice forked tongue

Rainbow sprinkle markings

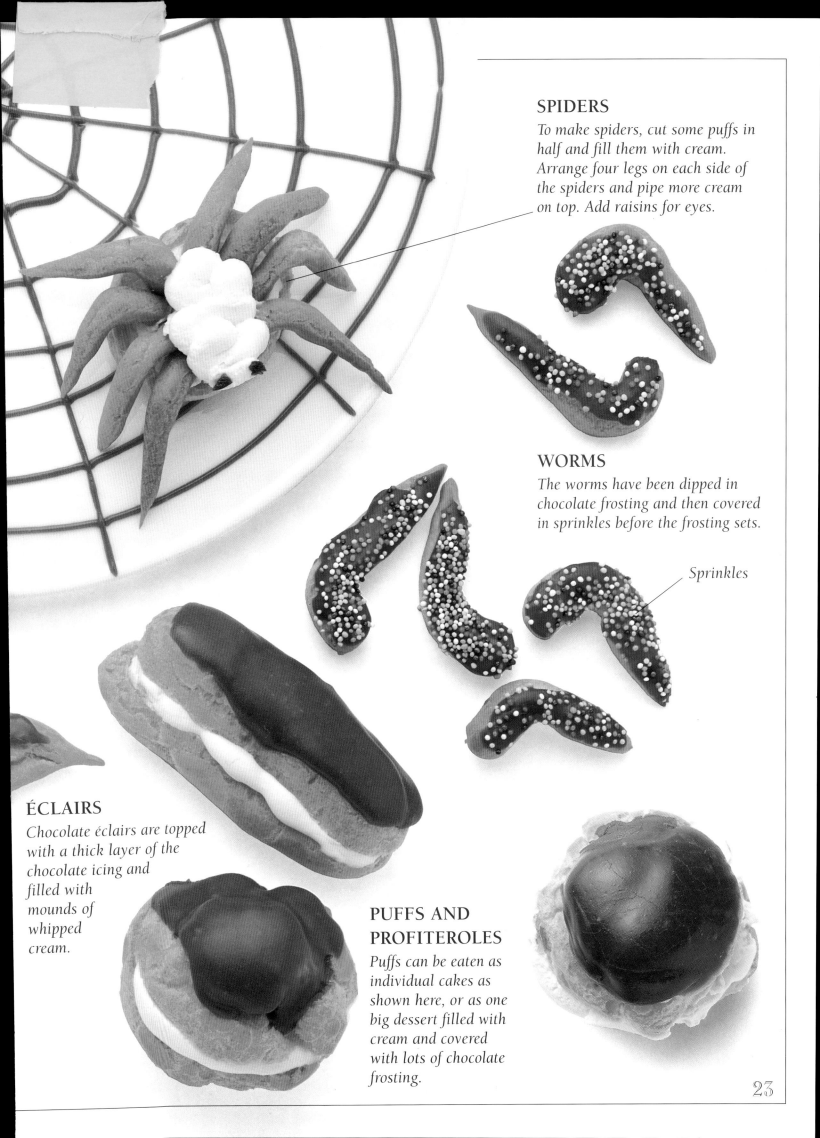

SPIDERS

To make spiders, cut some puffs in half and fill them with cream. Arrange four legs on each side of the spiders and pipe more cream on top. Add raisins for eyes.

WORMS

The worms have been dipped in chocolate frosting and then covered in sprinkles before the frosting sets.

Sprinkles

ÉCLAIRS

Chocolate éclairs are topped with a thick layer of the chocolate icing and filled with mounds of whipped cream.

PUFFS AND PROFITEROLES

Puffs can be eaten as individual cakes as shown here, or as one big dessert filled with cream and covered with lots of chocolate frosting.

23

FRUITY BREAD

A Christmas wreath not only tastes good but it also looks very festive ! Here you can see all you need to make a fruity bread wreath. The wreath will rise more quickly if you put it in an oiled plastic bag and then leave it in a warm place. Turn the page to see how to make the frosting and marzipan decoration for your wreath.

You will need

¼ cup (75 ml) warm milk

2 tablespoons (25 g) butter

1 egg

½ teaspoon salt

¼ cup (25 g) light brown sugar

1¼ cup (225 g) all-purpose flour

What to do

1 Set oven to 400°F (200°C). Put the sugar, flour, yeast, salt, spice, and cinnamon in the bowl and stir them together.

2 Add the butter and cut it up. Rub everything together with your fingertips until the mixture looks like fine breadcrumbs.

3 Add the fruit, egg, and milk. Mix them together to make a ball of dough. Knead the dough on a floured surface for five minutes.

1 envelope
instant yeast

1 heaping
tablespoon
candied citrus
peel

¼ cup (40 g) raisins

½ teaspoon
ground pie
spice

1 teaspoon ground cinnamon

COOK'S TOOLS

Pastry brush

Greased cookie sheet

Mixing bowl

Wire rack

Measuring cup

Knife

Wooden spoon

Spatula

4 Roll the dough into two
sausages about 24 in (60 cm)
long. Put the sausages side by side
and twist them together.

5 Bend the twist into a ring on
the cookie sheet. Wet the ends
of the twist with water and stick
them together.

6 Leave the ring in a warm place
until it has doubled in size.*
Bake it for 20 to 25 minutes, then
move it onto a wire cooling rack.

*This takes about 1 hour.

A Christmas Wreath

Turn your fruity wreath into a
Christmas treat with a tangy
lemon frosting and some
marzipan leaves and berries. If
you prefer, you can use the
fondant icing shown on page 8.

*1 oz (25g)
marzipan (for
holly leaves)*

*½ oz (15 g)
marzipan (for
holly berries)*

*1 tablespoon
lemon juice*

You will need

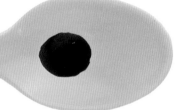

*12 drops
green food coloring*

12 drops red food coloring

*1½ cup 175 g
confectioners' sugar*

Coloring marzipan

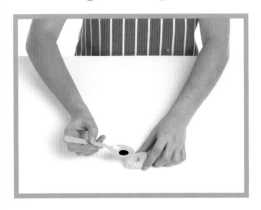

Make a hole with your finger in
the marzipan and add the food
coloring. Knead the marzipan
until it is an even colour.

Holly leaves

Roll the green marzipan out on a
sugared surface until it is ⅛ inch (3
mm) thick. Cut out leaves with the
cutter (or a knife).

Holly berries

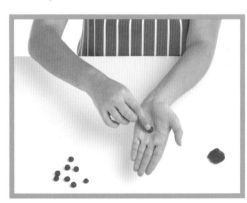

Take small pieces of red marzipan
and roll them into balls with your
fingers. Try to keep all the balls
the same size.

26

Making the frosting

COOK'S TOOLS

Small bowl

Sieve

Small holly leaf cookie cutters*

Rolling pin

Wooden spoon

1 Sift the confectioners' sugar into the bowl. Add the lemon juice and stir with the wooden spoon until the frosting is smooth.

2 Spoon the frosting along the top of the wreath and let it drip down the sides. Decorate the wreath before the frosting sets.

The finished Christmas wreath

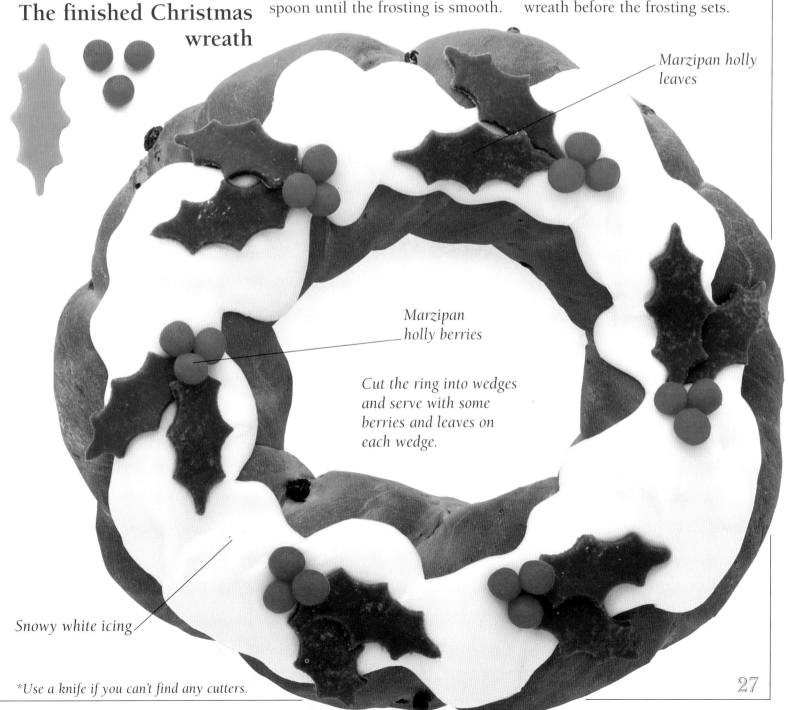

Marzipan holly leaves

Marzipan holly berries

Cut the ring into wedges and serve with some berries and leaves on each wedge.

Snowy white icing

*Use a knife if you can't find any cutters.

27

MAKING MERINGUES

Meringues are deliciously sweet and crunchy and are made from only the whites of eggs, some sugar, and a little salt. Separating the egg white from the yolk can be tricky because yolks break very easily, so always start with more eggs than you need! Be very careful not to allow any yolk to mix with the egg whites, or the recipe won't work. Meringues take five hours to cook because they have to be baked in a cool oven to keep them white. Start baking in the morning, so that you don't have to stay up all night!

COOK'S TOOLS

Cookie sheet

Small pitcher Cup Mixing bowl

Waxed paper

Teaspoon Spatula

Tablespoon Whisk

Small bowl Sharp knife Scissors

You will need

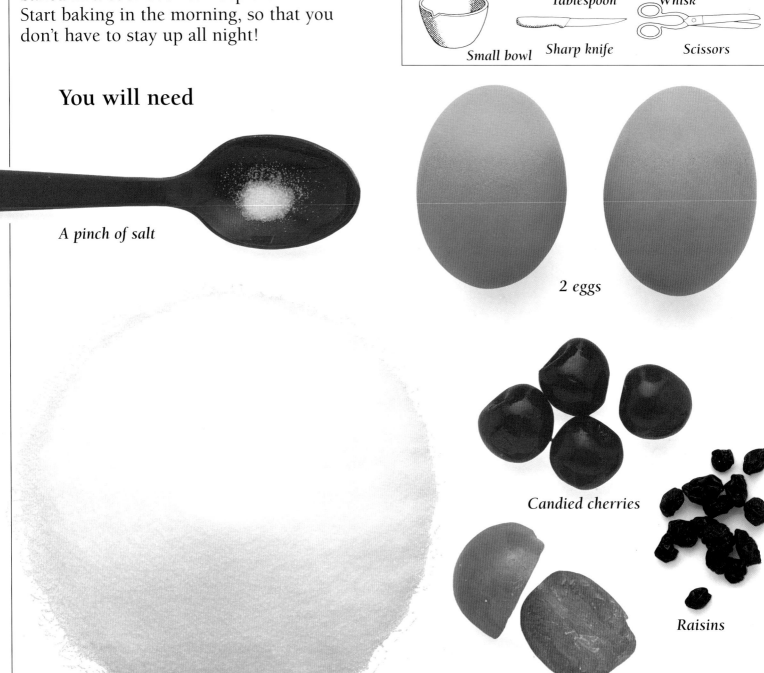

A pinch of salt

2 eggs

Candied cherries

Raisins

Candied orange peel

1½ cup (100 g) granulated sugar

28

What to do

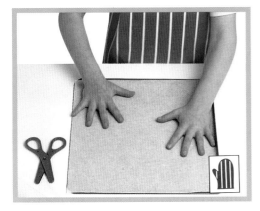

1 Set the oven at 225°F (107°C). Cover the cookie sheet with waxed paper or aluminum foil.

2 *Crack one egg in half and pour the yolk from one half of the shell into the other, letting the egg white fall into the pitcher.

3 Tip the yolk into the cup and the white into the small bowl. Do the same thing again to separate the second egg.

4 Add a pinch of salt to the egg whites in the small bowl. Beat the egg whites with the whisk until they form stiff peaks.

5 Whisk the sugar into the egg whites a little at a time, until you have used all the sugar and the meringue looks glossy.

Nests

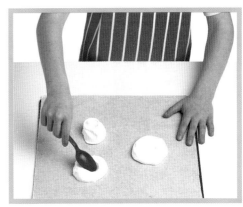

Shape a heaping tablespoonful of meringue into a circle on the cookie sheet. Make a hollow in the middle with a spoon.

Ghosts

Spread tablespoonfuls of meringue into ghost shapes with a teaspoon. Cut pieces of candied cherry to make eyes.

Snowmen

1 Use a teaspoonful of meringue for the head and a tablespoonful for the body. Decorate with pieces of raisin, candied peel, and cherry.

2 Bake the meringue ghosts, snowmen, and nests slowly for four to five hours until firm. Put them on a wire rack to cool.

*Ask an adult to help you with this.

SNOW-WHITE SURPRISES

Meringue nests make luscious desserts when they are filled with cream and fruit. Use canned fruit cocktail or fresh, soft fruits (like the ones shown here) and arrange them in pleasing designs on the cream-filled nests. You could make nests at Easter and fill them with chocolate eggs, or make ghosts for a Halloween treat. Snowmen are great as Christmas decorations that you can eat!

Canned pitted cherries

Canned mandarin orange segments

You will need

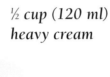

½ cup (120 ml) heavy cream

Seedless red and green grapes

Strawberries

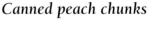

Filling the nests

Canned peach chunks

1 Pour the heavy cream into a small bowl. Whisk the cream until is thick and fluffy and forms soft peaks.

2 Cut off all the strawberry tops. Slice some of the strawberries and cut others into quarters with a sharp knife.*

3 Spoon the whipped cream into the nests and arrange the pieces of fruit in pretty patterns on top of them.

*Ask an adult to help you.

The finished meringues

MERINGUE NESTS

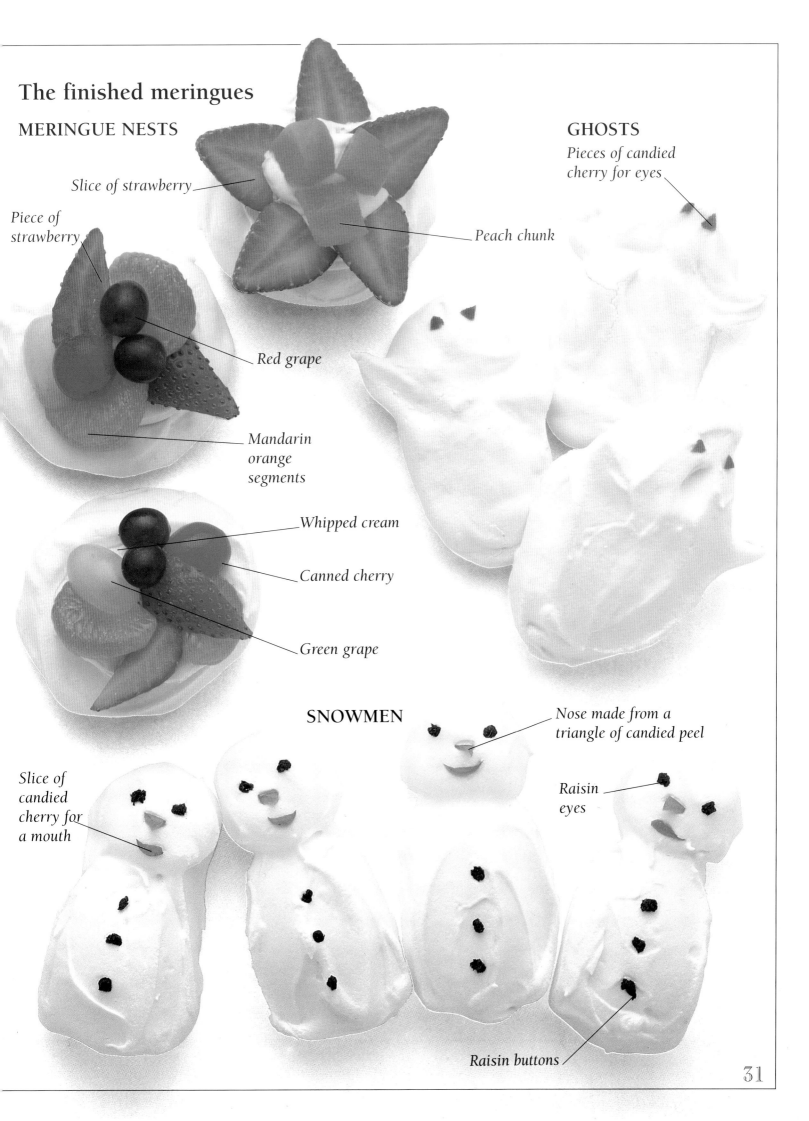

Slice of strawberry

Piece of strawberry

Red grape

Mandarin orange segments

Peach chunk

Whipped cream

Canned cherry

Green grape

GHOSTS

Pieces of candied cherry for eyes

SNOWMEN

Nose made from a triangle of candied peel

Slice of candied cherry for a mouth

Raisin eyes

Raisin buttons

31